Bayview

BEAUTIFUL THINGS
THAN BEYONCÉ

"Employing fierce language and eschewing fear of unflattering light, Parker (*Other People's Comfort Keeps Me Up at Night*) pays homage to the deep roots and collective wisdom of black womanhood."

—*Publishers Weekly*, **Starred Review**

"Parker weaves together Marvin Gaye lyrics, texting slang, and a critical, caring perspective on black womanhood to create poems that are both radically powerful and laugh-out-loud funny."

—*VICE*

"There are more beautiful things than Beyoncé in these pages because, as Morgan Parker writes in poems channeling the president's wife, the Venus Hottentot, and multiple Beyoncés: 'we're everyone. We have ideas and vaginas, history and clothes and a mother.' The kind of verve the late New York school Ted Berrigan would have called 'feminine marvelous and tough' is here, as well as the kind of vulnerability that fortifies genuine daring. This is a marvelous book. See for yourself. Morgan Parker is a fearlessly forward and forward-thinking literary star."

—**TERRANCE HAYES,**
winner of the National Book Award

"'Art hurts,' wrote poet Gwendolyn Brooks, 'Art urges voyages.' Morgan Parker's poems hurt deeply and voyage widely. They do not let you sit comfortably and idly and safe, but take you on an adventure like no other. Like the 'Fantastic Voyage' promised by R&B legends Lakeside, Parker's work is 'live, live, all the way live.' Get on board this trip; it is like no other."

—D. A. POWELL,
winner of the National Book Critics Circle Award

"Morgan Parker has a mind like wildfire and these pages are lit. I can't recall being this enthralled, entertained, and made alert by a book in a very long time."

—JAMI ATTENBERG,
New York Times best-selling
author of *The Middlesteins*

THERE ARE MORE BEAUTIFUL THINGS THAN BEYONCÉ

THERE ARE MORE BEAUTIFUL THINGS THAN BEYONCÉ

MORGAN PARKER

 TIN HOUSE BOOKS / Portland, Oregon & Brooklyn, New York

Copyright © 2017 Morgan Parker

Published by Tin House Books, Portland, Oregon, and Brooklyn, New York

Distributed by W. W. Norton & Company

Library of Congress Cataloging-in-Publication Data

Names: Parker, Morgan, author.
Title: There are more beautiful things than Beyoncé / Morgan Parker.
Description: Second U.S. edition. | Portland, OR : Tin House Books, 2017.
Identifiers: LCCN 2016049158 | ISBN 9781941040539 (softcover : acid-
    free paper)
Classification: LCC PS3616.A74547 A6 2017 | DDC 811/.6—dc23
LC record available at https://lccn.loc.gov/2016049158

Second U.S. Edition 2017
Printed in the USA
Interior design by Jakob Vala

www.tinhouse.com

Cover Art: Carrie Mae Weems
Portrait of a Woman Fallen from Grace, 1987
Gelatin silver print, 20 x 16 inches (print size)
© Carrie Mae Weems.
Courtesy of the artist and Jack Shainman Gallery, New York.

"The president is black / She black"

—KENDRICK LAMAR

CONTENTS

ALL THEY WANT IS MY MONEY
MY PUSSY MY BLOOD

I am free with the following conditions.

Give it up gimme gimme.

Okay so I'm Black in America right and I walk into a bar.

I drink a lot of wine and kiss a Black man on his beard.

I do whatever I want because I could die any minute.

I don't mean YOLO I mean they are hunting me.

I know my pussy is real good because they said so.

I say to my friend I am broke as a joke.

I am Starvin' Like Marvin Gaye.

I'm so hungry I could get it on.

There's far too many of me dying.

The present is not so different.

Everybody looks like everybody I worked with.

Everybody looks like everybody I kissed.

Men champion men and animals.

Everybody thinks I'm going to die.

At the museum I tell the school group about Black art.

I tell them the word *contemporary*.

I have a nose ring I forget about.

I have a brother and he is also Black.

I am a little modern to a fault.

I say this painting is contemporary like you and me.

They ask me about slavery. They say Martin Luther King.

At school they learned that Black people happened.

The present is not so different.

I'm looking into their Black faces.

They do not understand that they exist.

I'm Black in America and I walk

into a bar and drink a lot of wine, kiss a white man on his beard.

There is no indictment.

I could die any minute of depression.

I just want to have sex most of the time.

I just want my student loans to disappear.

I just want to understand my savings account.

What is happening to my five dollar one cent.

I am free with the following conditions.

What is happening to my brother.

What if I do something wrong.

My blood is so hot and wet right now.

I know they want it.

I do everything right just in case.

I don't want to give away my money but here I am.

It's so stupid I have to say here I am.

They like to be on top.

I am being set up.

I am a tree and some fruits are good and some are bad.

The President Has Never Said the Word *Black*

To the extent that one begins
to wonder if he is broken.

It is not so difficult to open
teeth and brass taxes.

The president is all like
five on the bleep hand side.

The president be like
we lost a young   boy today.

The pursuit of happiness
is guaranteed for all fellow   Americans.

He is nobody special like us.
He says brothers and sisters.

What kind of bodies are movable
and feasts. What color are visions.

When he opens his mouth
a chameleon is inside, starving.

Hottentot Venus

I wish my pussy could live
in a different shape and get
some goddamn respect.
Should I thank you?
Business is booming
and I am not loved
the way I want to be.
I am an elastic
winter: sympathy
and shock, addictive
decoration. In the sunlight
my captors
drink African
hibiscus. They tell me
I look regal bearing fruit.
I am technically nothing
human.
I will never be
a woman.
Somewhere in my
memory, I was held
by a man who said
I deserved it.
Now I understand.

No one worries about me
because I am getting paid.
I am here to show you
who you are, to cradle
your large skulls
and remind you
you are perfect. Mother America,
unleash your sons.
Everything beautiful, you own.

Another Another Autumn
in New York

When I drink anything
out of a martini glass
I feel untouched by
professional and sexual
rejection. I am a dreamer
with empty hands and
I like the chill.
I will not be attending the party
tonight, because I am
microwaving multiple Lean Cuisines
and watching *Wife Swap*,
which is designed to get back
at fathers, as westernized media
is often wont to do.
I don't know
when I got so punk rock
but when I catch
myself in the mirror I
feel stronger. So when
at five in the afternoon
something on my TV says
time is not on your side
I don't give any

shits at all. Instead I smoke
a joint like I'm
a teenager and eat a whole
box of cupcakes.
Stepping on leaves I get
first-night thrill.
Confuse the meanings
of castle and slum, exotic
and erotic. I bless
the dark, tuck
myself into a canyon
of steel. I breathe
dried honeysuckle
and hope. I live somewhere
imaginary.

Poem on Beyoncé's Birthday

Drinking cough syrup from a glass shaped
Like your body I wish was mine but as dark
As something in my mind telling me
I'm not woman enough for these days
Colored with reddish loathing
Which feels, to me, more significant than sun
My existence keeps going
Ripple in other people's mouths
Pools of privilege and worship
I want, I keep thinking
I am exclusively post-everything
Animals licking my chin, new leaves stretching
From a palm plant like a man's greedy arms
Today your open eyes are two fresh buds
Anything could be waiting.

Lush Life

The most beautiful hearse   I have ever seen
is parked in front of my stoop
Perched   hands folded for six to eight weeks
twinkling like a siren   a new idea of love

Trees are planted but don't exist yet
They are leaning non existent   into us
A trough of hearts meets me in the anxious sun
I could rot here

Something like   the holy spirit
pours you over bruised ice
There isn't anything   more to say than holy
Beautiful men never looking upon me

I take music self-stirred   and sleep
alone   curve into the morning like an almond
My shoulders   lush as romantics
You wash up on a barstool
smooth heartache   black sand

Beyoncé on the Line for Gaga

Girl you know you ain't that busy.
Without me   you're just two ears
stuffed with glitter.
          Spoken gun   your name
baby's first words when she enters
          swag up   covered in
gunmetal spandex, cigarettes for eyes.
Say my name, louder
          come into   these hips
and live. Let
platform heels tightrope curves,
          make Jiggaman jealous.
He runs the streets
I pour into them, weave first
fierce nymph of Texas
          holy in black.
You feel me? This booty
is smooth running water.
I shake   too thick for love,
push records like dimes,
rep the hustle   slick as legs.
I know you like that.
          I carry the hood up in this bling.

Soft brown fingers
got rocks for days. Lips glossed opening
    for a special purpose.
You say *Tell 'em B*
I open my legs, throw my shades on like,
Divas gettin' money.   Hard as the boys.
Give me all
your little monsters and I will burn them up.
Give me your hand
and I will let you back this up.
Tonight   I make a name for you.

We Don't Know When We Were Opened (Or, The Origin of the Universe)

after Mickalene Thomas

A sip of liquor from a creek. Saturday syndicated
Good Times, bare legs, colors draped like
an afterthought. We   bright enough to blind you.
Dear anyone, dear high-heel metronome, white
noise, hush us shhhhh, hush us. We're artisanal
crafts, rare gems, bed of leafy bush you call
us   superfood. Jeweled lips, we're rich
We're everyone. We have ideas and vaginas,
history and clothes and a mother. Portrait-ready
American blues. Palm trees and back issues
of *JET*, pink lotion, gin on ice, zebras, fig lipstick.
One day we learned to migrate. One day we studied
Mamma making her face. Bright new brown, scent of Nana
and cinnamon. Shadows of husbands and vineyards,
records curated to our allure, incense, unconcern.
Champagne is how the Xanax goes down, royal blue
reigning. We're begging anyone not to forget
we're turned on with control. We better homes and gardens.
We real grown. We garden of soiled panties.
            We low hum of satisfaction. We is is is is is is is
    touch, touch, shine, a little taste. You're gonna
                            give us the love we need.

My Vinyl Weighs a Ton

Sit down shut up slip me out of my sleeve.
I have come from the grasses of California.

Twenty years of the dark I carry.
The sun bends its back over Struggle City.

It hits me first thing: I've never been cool.
I am driving with glass eyes and lead feet.

I jetpack into the heaviness alone.
My bare face hanging out all over the kitchen counter.

What's largest is the ego, half animal growing near mint.
I'm a rare EP strutting into the brown morning.

T-shirts are a theme. The neighborhood watches.
Lawn chairs tumble into liquor stores alone.

The good old urban sprawl at half volume.
It is literally just another day.

All my friends are changing religions and getting laid.
I have been too patient.

It's just one long slumber party in here. It seems impossible
that Mom will ever arrive, car running, to take me home.

Beyoncé Is Sorry for What She Won't Feel

The capital's so icy, I see my
perfect breath. It looks like a body
on its knees. Most days I strut
my figure on lock. A Nation
of Weaves assembles at my
Jimmy Choos, gazes into green light
and falls asleep. First Lady of desire,
I pant for our future. Like America
and wine, I am all legs. A sheepskin
bleached and dyed, left in the sun.
Dear Sunday you are a rash like
tresses falling to shoulders, pink
highlights humming the sky
like a tease. How do you feel
in moonrise, the stomach growl
of life slowly closing? Do you wonder
about escape, the blank, quiet frontier?
I mouth *Free* and *Home* into a crowd
but they only hear gold extensions.
I listen for prophecies
from my daughter's sticky mouth.
While I pick her hair, she cries.
I say, Never give them
what they want, when they want it.

Afro

I'm hiding secrets & weapons in there: buttermilk
pancake cardboard, boxes of purple juice, a magic word
our Auntie Angela spoke into her fist & released into
hot black evening like gunpowder or a Kool, 40 yards of
cheap wax prints, *The Autobiography of Malcolm X*, a Zulu
folktale warning against hunters drunk on Polo shirts &
Jägermeister, blueprints for building ergonomically perfect
dancers & athletes, the chords to what would have been
Michael's next song, a mule stuffed with diamonds &
gold, Miss Holiday's vocal cords, the jokes Dave Chapelle's
been crafting off the grid, sex & brown liquor intended
for distribution at Sunday schools in white suburbs, or in
other words exactly what a white glove might expect to
find taped to my leg & swallowed down my gullet & locked
in my trunk & fogging my dirty mind & glowing like
treasure in my autopsy

These Are Dangerous Times, Man

Do you know what I would do
with the glory of everyone?
I would set it on my tongue.
I've been meaning to sing this
against chamomile hissing
up from the grates.
Not because it is
dark but because of how
I interpret the rules.
While tree trunks
grow into their pleats,
I continue to respect
unwritten codes.
The world would crumble
without my unwavering
sacrifice. I try to write
a text message
to describe
all my feelings
but the emoticon hands
are all white.
White Whine.
White flowers in a river.
Some plantation
stuck in my teeth like a seed.

I think the phone is racist.
The phone
doesn't care about Black people.
The phone is the nation
that loves the phone.
Otherwise my feelings are unable
to be expressed.
A white thumb pointed down.
You are
everything good.
I suck color
out of the night and then
your finger bones.
We become
a beautiful collection
of knots
trembling on the floor.
I need to know
what it feels like to be softened.
Tender filet on a fresh
wood block.
Small, warm body
in a field, un-itching.
Our bodies
never synchronized
enough.

Rebirth of Slick

& sashayed
& solar   I'm a moodless seedling
on the day Jay Z was born
& Fred Hampton was killed

Watching TV & thinking "White people are crazy"
Watching YouTube & thinking "Kanye West
is crazy"
Looking in the mirror

Everything crazy is the best
It's what I learned from aunties
& empty bottles after midnight
The birth of a bullshitter
        in dark lipstick & big dreams

It's easy to be ravishing: don't think
I am feeling smooth & twirl my wrist as such
Flock to me I ain't scared
My bed is a cross between dancehall & fruit field
Everyone is on the list   plus infinity

I was born this way: unsatisfied
My color is a bridge with no other side
In a second life my voice is a drum kit
Reigning over green hills like weather
    I am king & anthem
    I know how to relax

RoboBeyoncé

Charging in the darkroom
while you sleep I am touch and go
I flicker and get turned on
Exterior shell, interior disco
I like my liver steeled
as a gun, my wires
unbuttoned to you
The reason I was built
is to outlast some terribly
feminine sickness
that is delivered
to the blood through kale
salad and pity and men
with straight-haired girlfriends
The future's a skirt of
expectation to mourn
This way, hard-cased
you can put your eyes on me
It's less about obedience than
silvery lipstick stains
It's mostly about machine tits
Artificially I'm interested
Virtually I'm drunk
The future's a girlish helmet

with circuits that need doctors
In the future our bodies can't
I dare you
Tell me apart from other girls
Nothing aches in here
It's a quiet, calculated shame

Delicate and Jumpy

Turns out I feel my body
more than I should. My eyes dart

like a small animal. I'm a museum
of necklines and cloudscapes, a heaven

diving into the wrong hard mountain.
Soon a beer-colored sky will sneak

up behind the fence. I toss my hair
to the street without permission.

A couple in matching pea coats smokes
electronic cigarettes across the platform.

I am a tiny robot like them
but there is no one to love my robo-heart.

On the last day of the year I enter
a scalding tub and think you away.

It is too cold and too quiet for me
to sign language the sky.

Right now six people are in outer space,
and you are growing smaller in my mind.

I just want to have a heart for this, to be
a shaved dog, begging at your heels.

Freaky Friday Starring Beyoncé and Lady Gaga

for example
I'd miss my booty
in your butt
would hate
to reach back
and find history
borrowed not branded
would miss my glitz in your glam
my rhythm in your rock
you'd take me as a cold black cape
while I relax into your fishnets
the secret is
I'm a body for anyone
to fill
in you I light
a candle
for you
which is me
slip a flower into our hair
listen to our body
yours and mine
its sniveling crawl
down the block its beat

and I in your short strut
take comfort in good
white reason
who'd want   enter this
whose breasts
as heavy to touch
whose vogue so viewed
and blocked
we'd kill
for solace
bodiced to despair
I'd smear black
lipstick on your thin lips
try to forget
I ever belonged in you
I'd see easier
and you would hold
my body upright
gut the throat
find out what comes up
          you'd see
I'm just a slab of something

13 Ways of Looking at a Black Girl

at risk   pretty   Queen Latifah   Nikki Giovanni
   Ma   Tina Turner   sex
dyke   ugly   bitch   sex   Mamma   NeNe Leakes
Sally Hemings   THOT   Erykah Badu   easy
bipolar   Beyoncé   sex   kitchen   rape
   wifey   Nina Simone   Nicki Minaj
   sex   sex   Whitney Houston
Toni Morrison   I am hungry   for myself
         Grace Jones   diva   slut
thong   darkie   Michelle Obama
   high yellow   nappy   flawless   Audre Lorde
Lena Horne   lips   Sandra Bland   sex   strong
sex   sister   Wanda Sykes   sassy   witch
low-income   sex   booty
   well-spoken   Issa Rae   less
hotep   beautiful   Hottentot Venus   sex
   chickenhead   thick   Alice Walker   queen
   dead   sex   just a friend
Shonda Rhimes   trouble   sick   sex   mean
   hair   bell hooks   single
dying   tragic
sex   help   carefree   chocolate
   special   exotic   sex   ratchet
      Felicia   loud   lost

The Book of Negroes

1
Summertime and the living is
extraordinarily difficult. The sunset

seems unimportant. It becomes
a calm. Sunglasses, white

wine spritzers. Would you hate yourself
less if you picked your fruit from trees.

You prefer friends to remain
in train stations. What side the mountain

is home. You were not invited
into the orange groves.

Sometimes you go outside
and control is possible.

Everybody has an opinion.
Everything rolls off your shoulders.

2
This book is spit, cum, cloud cover.
We   Definite people.

This book is about lying down quietly.
No one wrote the blessing of our ankles

in foamy water. We always emerge.
We sing because we cannot bear the heat.

We wear black. We cannot bear the heat.
We don't call the police. We fill bathtubs with

windchimes and lower them in the ground.
We   Nothing left.

This book is uncorrected proof. You read it
on your eyelids. You sleep under it.

You give it away. You tear out whole chapters.
You say you read it but you didn't.

3
You see the commercial on BET
while you're painting your nails.

The women are only crying.
The slave cabins are dull. You're trying

to text this dude: *Negro, please,*
why sleep when the world so bad.

For him you would be pumice shined to pearl.
He makes you wanna write your name.

Everybody has an opinion.
You shiver and it is permission.

You are beautiful because you're funny.
You are alive because you're a question.

The Gospel According to Her

What to a slave is the fourth of july.
What to a woman is a vote.
What to a slave is river water.
What to a slave is an award show.
What to a slave is fine china.
What to a woman is a canopy bed.
What to a slave is the hard sky.
What to a woman is please.
What to a woman is the bottom of a glass.
What to a slave are flatlands from an aircraft.
What to a woman is permission.
What to a woman is the milky way.
What to a slave is a square technically it's perfect.

Black Woman with Chicken

after Carrie Mae Weems

High in my
stomach there
you are, phantom
of a flat sea. I never
should have grown
up before
your eyes. I'm the
sparkle on
glass lips.
Type A
in the kitchen wanting
more. Blurry
princess, self-narrating.
For my
name I took
the shells
offered & spit
out your
bones with
wondrous glut.
I have more
eyelids than anyone
I know. No rest
for the sweet
& lowdowns

but me when I'm
salted &
nightcapped I
arrive at the steps
of an eerie
castle, black
& white
a church
have I been
here before have I
been me before &
turned my
back to myself.
Long black dress.
I'm what you want.
If you don't
like what you
see, remember
I'm only
a figment, screen
of hunger & pining.
A spook
& you
feast your eyes

The Gospel of Jesus's Wife

Good morning how may I
offend you on this cracked
open Sabbath Dear God
I promise to prop you up
Of course I exist
I have every small name
Metaphorically draped in linen
I am often used to describe
the invisible how it carries
I answer your phone and pack
your lunches for it is written
A woman must
A man shall receive
Scrolling through profile pics I am
ashamed I disappear into
mysterious pastures
O unproven halo
Have I ever lived
I must be a joke
written in seething
sweat after the passage
of eternal lives
snapped broomsticks
To dusting I return singing

Jesus loves me yes
Yes and my body
My steepled temple
O God your flesh is a word
My flesh by the grace of you
I believe in everything
Brown bodies in a salty river
Your praises in their swollen cheeks
I must be the B-side
clipped to the editing floor
A gold road paved with me
And Jesus said medium rare
And I bowed quietly eternally
Cleaned his cup on my apron
and poured him his blood
In this parable I am the goblet
Crater of birth and service
I leave no trace
I become the smallest book
Smooth vellum pages
Anciently flaking
With these thorns I thee stroke
and lie down under questions
Jesus what can you offer me

Will you return from your journey
across skin-colored sands
to wash the feet of other women
and touch my head with truth
I will be waiting in a doorframe until harvest
Until the sky is so clear I see
my lipstick reflecting in the olive trees
Take the fever out of me
Come in and rise again and again

White Beyoncé

Sneezed on the beat
and blessed her self

Her love goes viral her love
of teeth and starched collar

Her husband is a baseball cap
She shakes his hand good night

She tips a bowing manicurist
who thinks she's president

Her daughter is at the academy
wrongly pronouncing Spanish

She watches Turner Classic Movies
and sees herself there

Up in da country club she dines with friends
The conversation is breezy

Doesn't look the waiter in the eyes
ordering vegan chicken salad w/ amenities

She sees into her past
The conversation is breezy

She's been in the dictionary since
she was born her words Victorian highways

She's un-revolutionarily flawless
Feminist-approved she vacations daily

She woke up like a million bucks
slipped into lacy panties it's always sunny

Her husband is upstanding of course
The tabs call him Mr.

She performs and the coverage is breezy:
What rosy cheeks what milky vacancy

Her daughter learns about beauty
Discovers nothing surprising

The President's Wife

Sometimes I wonder
Is Beyoncé who she says she is
Will I accidentally live forever
And be sentenced to smile at men
I wish were dead
Is loneliness cultural
Are lips true
Is a mother still a self
Do I glow in the dark
What if men are wrong
And English isn't sound blue isn't color
Eyes are the window to storm
Am I too transparent in this skirt suit
Is the skirt suit a social construct
What does money cost
Should I stop talking while the ocean
Takes California hot breath takes the capital
Will ritual outlast what visits
Sleeping daughters with bad words
What lets some girls grow warm and tall
The arms of their lovers
Are rich and imaginary like me
Is desire making me sick
Building in my organs like ammunition

Tiptoeing behind my eyes until
I'm digital I'm static
Is it called desire can it speak
What does beautiful cost do I afford it
Do I roll off the tongue
Is America going to be sick
Will fat kids inherit the earth
Will you untag me from that picture
Do you think I should cut my bangs
Do I have any friends
Do you believe in me
Should I go to sleep
Try again harder tomorrow
Should I answer the phone
Who is it
Who want the world like it is
Spoke Baraka can you hear him now
Do you understand
Are calories and sitcoms
Here to make me sad
Am I a moon no one sees
Does my lipstick look okay
Am I growing tired
Of my alternative lifestyle

Or would I like a fresh glass
Is there something spectacular
In fallen trees ancient hieroglyphs
Hippie towns twentysomethings will they
Save us
Is it possible to disappear
What's it like to be the first anything

Welcome to the Jungle

With champagne I try expired white ones
I mean pills I mean men

I think I'm going crazy sometimes really
you think I'm joking I'm never joking

All Men Have Been Created Equally
To Shiver At The Thought Of Me

is something I used to think but forgot
or got drunk tried smoking something new

put on a wig made a scene threw up
in someone's living room cooked

too much food every time can someone just
give it to me when I get home

I know the answer is probably cleavage
cleavage all the boys I know

holding my arms down taking off
my bracelets with their white hands

I've pissed on a sidewalk in midtown watched
a Joan Crawford movie at dawn

art is nice but the question is how are you
making money are you for sale

people in movies are always saying
I can't live like this! packing a little bag

or throwing down their forks I mean it
one of these days my whole body might just

go away like just standing in line
at Whole Foods or purgatory I wish I were

a dream for you to suck on
once I got four tattoos

cut off all my hair
dyed my hair blonde

had a party had fifty parties
looked for Jupiter and Venus in the smog

painted and repainted my nails
what can they do for you sir

the question is where the fuck
is the sun the answer is tiptoe

into the park at midnight pretend
it's green like home

Beyoncé, Touring in Asia, Breaks Down in a White Tee

This one goes out to
the time of night when
cheeks up against
lamé   we pose
& come hither with long acrylic
let them   all y'all
        come to us   holler
when moon rises peach
over Mom's kitchen table
some grasses bending
                homegirl way

if you could see me now   arms up
over the mantel   or on my back
pink heels in the air   what's not
to love?

you think
        you're something
special shawty   what your name is?
sometimes you change
        winter it's like this
honey   we need the machines to live

you know me because   you are
the broken chest
        where first syllable   cut
& bloomed   where mascara
        finally catches
we have
no time for lights
we have   our throats our skin

I just love my fans so much
            this is how much

What Beyoncé Won't Say on a Shrink's Couch

what if I said I'm tired
and they heard wrong
said *sing it*

Ain't Misbehavin'

I take a sip of beer.
My asshole feels.
I cannot believe
in how successful
and how alone I have been
today. I spend
most nights topless
and appreciate
my dog. I go to sleep clutching
the side of the bed.
I blow my nose
and repent for the night
before. I masturbate.
Remember the album
that mattered when we
were still poor?
Persons say
I'm getting along
just fine. Like I'm
a baby who
just claps and shits.
Some stars have aligned
in our spines. Moons conjuncting
my eye shadow flushing,

planets up to their necks
in our longing. Without your
stringy hair in cushions,
stomach against
the upcoming
morning traffic noise I
get bored. No one to walk with
into the glowing couch, the green
afterward. I am saving for you
a sharpened arrowhead
for luck and practicality.

Untitled While Listening to Drake

That summer you only listened to
Versions of *The Girl from Ipanema*
Drank Vinho Verde and chopped cherry tomatoes like
You were an extra in a *Mad Men* vacation scene
You were gaining weight in your thighs
Ashamed to have sex or go to the beach
You couldn't see yourself
Blushing in the smoke
Sometimes it was so sunny you thought
You would die or even worse live to be old
And still collecting dogs like sunrises
Waking up thinking today is the day
Today is not the day
Isn't wine so wonderful more than men
Isn't the sun what you can't have
Because you have feelings you need to see a doctor
The doctor says you will never know the truth
She offers you all the tissues and hot tea you like
When you are finished ignoring her you go to dinner
You order bibimbap in the hot pot and gaze into fried egg
You're listening to a friend and disappointed
The train ride home is long and cold
That summer the music was so perfect and incorrect
Throat filling with accidents

It was like you didn't have power but were lifted
With large strange hands from one day to another
Meanwhile you were sleeping
You were so tired
What strange dreams and sweaty sheets
The disorientation of waking
The gloom of being where you are meant to be
It's how mice are trapped alone
Your idea of being in love only a sound

Beyoncé in Third Person

I type Beyoncé into my phone
five out of seven days a week.
That's because I am a woman.
I'm a little unpolished
behind the scenes. I am lonely
and so are all my friends.
When one season of
The Real Housewives closes,
another one opens. New moons
disappear unmagically. I am very
complicated and so is Beyoncé.
Dogs in their gait of privilege
circle her. Snow falls for her,
shellacks windows for her.
Beyoncé, are you sure you're okay?
I slice lemons in my quiet apartment
and pile them on a step. When I think
about revolution, I turn to the B-side
of *Dangerously in Love*. I sequin
my breasts like morning
shells, teeth sucked as performance.
People say things
they think are true, like "I love you"
and "I feel in a particular way."

I want to be so close and bold.
In the news today Beyoncé went
to brunch this weekend. Two
neighborhoods over, dressed in all black.
Comparing salad recipes
and third-wheeling weekend dinners
dog kibble in my loafers
seducing my self in sweat pants
is not how I envisioned my twenties
or is it. In high school I made a mixtape
called "Ladies Is Pimps Too."
That was long before my therapist
asked about my masculinity
while new buds in Riverside Park
slobbered with rain.
The only dream I've had all year
is the one where I am driving
out of control. The brakes are shot,
the landscape changes, accelerate
instead of stop. It's almost too
obvious to interpret, like teeth
or pomegranates, or ocean.
If you aren't interested in self-
absorption, do not follow me

on Twitter. Sometimes I think
I should have been left
in the incubator longer.
Everyone got high
levels of entitlement in our veins.
We think we are owed.
Everything, but especially silence.
A secret is during commercials
I am living other lives, sautéing
green vegetables, imagining spring
breeze carry me through the apartment
like a branch, or a painter. There is
no humor in touch, the absolute truth.
If I breathed on Beyoncé, would she
begin to weep? I go to sleep,
it's dark, no one breathes.

Heaven Be a Xanax

When people say how are you
I say good
It is a rule no one can answer
Crying in the Gap by my therapist's office
or I am still angry with my parents
for traumatizing me
through organized sports
Dangerous and satisfying body of water
I can almost remember heaven
or Still a woman slaughtered for wonder
or Unfortunately misplaced grip
I am not doing a good job waiting
When I get to heaven I'm going
to wear my good bra
so no one can stay mad at me
I won't have any feelings to hurt just
cheeseburgers on cheeseburgers on
deep colored slumber
Just men offering their golden bodies
And I will take the offering on my tongue
And it will not be a vault
And someone will not invade me
And I will kneel to pray
And I will address the prayer to myself
And I will be allowed

Beyoncé Celebrates
Black History Month

I have almost
forgotten my roots
are not long
blonde. I have almost forgotten
what it means to be at sea.

Earth, Wind & Fire Reunion Tour 2013

Everything's exactly like old times
Just like I will always fear

The level of psychology this week
High as yellow butterflies stroking my knee

I would say transformation
White linen leaks from my throat

Greetings I hope this finds you well
Ignoring the size of the moon and kissing

Almost-rain gives up on the concrete
Unwhole but close enough   unanchored

Tornado singing a song in skin casing
& bell-bottoms carrying absolutely everything

A people rolls too deep to count the dark pupils
One nation under smooth hot storm

Part Joplin, part Jackson, kiss of Curtis
We stay here prophetic

Aching suburban, sweating with the camaraderie
Of early works   I stand for the fire

I see a shivering boogie in the sky like thunder
O make me the leather fringe of your sleeve

It's hard to believe love is anything but
Full breasts, a hot biscuit, and a flute

Please come sit with me in the reeds
I'm too small to see but I'm listening

It's Getting Hot in Here So Take Off All Your Clothes

All day men shout like lizards, sharp-tongued
in the desert for salty flies. The sky's the boss
of us: I can't spit when I try. In the heat, less
is everything: respect, power, mouths, sex.
All of it is taken from me. I step into a volcano
& melt like the witch I am. I want to be flawed

all the way to bed. Wake up, flawless.
Subjected, flawless. Swallowed my tongue
for communion. I mean, volcano.
I erupt with a mouth like a bossy
eagle. I made my bed so I have sex
in it. My body gets more for less

& O! When I say less
I mean as in classically beautiful, flaws
spilling out of my mouth like sexy
moon rocks. I cut out men's tongues &
I sharpen myself & I'm scary & I'm bossy:
I'm the chick who raises snakes like a volcano

spews its desert under pressure. Volcanic
in the streets & volcanic in the bed. Less
kitchenware, more potent libidos bossing
men around. All day they shout, flaws
on my crystal. All day I feel their tongues.
It's literal, it isn't sexual.

Okay maybe it is about sex.
What passes for magic. How a sleeping volcano
is still a volcano. How with my tongue
I turn on a light like God & I have less
privilege than God. How even with flaws
under these clothes I could be the boss

of you without them. Magic. Boss
you all night long. & of course I mean sex
but I mean teaching, too. Black girl rage, flawless.
This diamond my diamond in a volcano's
hot, lost city. & I do not mean helpless.

Take a Walk on the Wild Side

I drink fewer martinis and watch more
movies   you would like it here
Cardboard skyline   deeply in my chest
I feel the bass you-know-where   exactly
Self-portrait of early June
Consider me a luminous rooftop
Soundtrack Black bossanova
Palm tree tears
Velvet robes & blue
eye shadow you're only a shrug
I'm older now than the hot girls
Think about that, babe
Still considering my eyebrows   but no heart
to touch them Fussing with plum
lip color & loose panty hose I'm probably
going to impress you
Old-fashioned with thigh-high split I am hoping to be
    your eternal world
Bending to extract a pie   my mind sticks to you
like a bad feminist   or someone
deranged   hands backside-first to apron
downer cigarette
You'll marry me but I'll be goddamned
Without you my mouth becomes my face

My thighs lock into absence
Departure & terminal I'm probably going to impress you
Los Angeles genesis
Black & white 20th century hard-on
If we touch we enter to the world   Please let me
And the colored girls go:

The Book of Revelation

Kiss the years, their filth: it's my turn
To dress up forlorn in gold, fib

Through rotting teeth
I'm looking regal, constantly exploding

Do you think I could be a witch
Can shine be caught like a fever

My therapist says something
In my core is dark and the surface of my planet too

She says *Many creative people*
& I can't see a beautiful day if I tried

She says peace is something
people tell themselves

99 Problems

1. Playing *house* I was adopted
2. or the dog
3. I understood
4. They made me the wild creek
   between *Class Clown* & *Most Unique*
5. The chocolate _____
6. One afternoon the dog killed
   a bird in our garage
7. He brought it to my feet
8. In the Bible every wing is real
9. I could be a witch
10. Dating
11. Dating
12. It is impossible to always be touching
13. Two-hundred-fiddy to unpack this
14. Sixty a bag to heal
15. Inhale/heal
16. Oppression
17. Oppression
18. Oppression
19. Oppression
20. Defense
21. Teaching
22. Listening

23. Never knew him
24. Nana packed the slow car alone
25. Picked six honey-heads from school
26. Drove 'til the sky turned
27. a new state
28. I don't know anything else
29. It doesn't matter
30. I wake up not
    sure I want to
31. I don't know how to explain
    every wish is an ice cube
    I swallow whole
32. It is important for me to say I'm OK
33–35. Fucked a white boy
36–42. American History
43. *Where are you from?*
44. Prozac Weight
45. Thomas and I got pulled over
    in Bed-Stuy last Saturday night
46. We were in the back of a cab
47. Taxes
48. The wilting planet
49. Sometimes I forget to take my pills
50. I do it on purpose

51. I can't feel anything
52. A clean body like a lake
        I'm some shit bodies sunk into
53. Prison Industrial Complex
54. Nonprofit Industrial Complex
55. Marriage Industrial Complex
56. Landlords
57. Nigger
58. OKCupid
59. White Saviors
60. Karaoke
61. Limited cocktail shrimps
62–70. *Please check all that apply: panic attacks hopelessness decreased socialization guilt general overwhelming stress suicide attempts*
71. *Are you OK?*
72. Tyler Perry
73. Hangovers
74. The Western concept of Time
75. Food Deserts
76. James Franco
77. OK I drank too much
78. again
79. It is impossible to always be taking a lavender bath

80. Men at intersections
81. Men in smoky formations
82. Men in the waiting room
83. Men at Popeyes
84. Men up my skirt
85. Mercury Retrograde
86. My dog eats a lipstick
87. Subjectivity
88. *No*
89. *Where are you from?*
90. Lost records
91. My real name
92. Fitting in
93. Uninterested sex
94. Teacher called me Sheila
95. Sheila was the other Black girl
96. Sheila hated me
97. What we mean by "come up"
98. *Be strong*
99. I'm tired

Slouching Toward Beyoncé

Who reads her horoscope
in secret and bathes
her loose strings
in holy watercolor, cucumbers
over the temple. Her body
is like mine it is filled
with holes. It starts black
and stays   Black.
      I keep thinking
      the only city left
      is outer space
          where we lived
          before
      we had tongues.
Things don't fall
apart they find new homes.
Down here there's a thing
called skin   I keep mine clean.
There are things
called *medication*
and *days*.   They are hard
to believe. I am tired
so I wife myself.
      Down here

the boys are theoretical.
I shrink their hearts. I say spells because
I'm magic.   Fire
is another word for absolute
sunset on a high cliff.
I am never afraid to jump.
O Beyoncé   I love you
your fragments like a map.
I think I am addicted.
You soaked blue   you trouble
in my sight. The beast has come
at last: hair of a cattail
and legs of a palm.
The truth like a bowl of seeds.
The secret album. Midnight.
O! Vessel of womanhood
I am loosed upon the world
with dust and filed nails.
All my life I turn water into wine.
This the hour   I lower my shoulders.
My second coming: split
screen, clouds like orchid
        bulbs in the throat.

Let Me Handle My Business, Damn

Took me awhile to learn the good words

make the rain on my window grown

and sexy now I'm in the tub holding down

that on-sale Bordeaux pretending

to be well-adjusted I am on that real

jazz shit sometimes I run the streets

sometimes they run me I'm the body

of the queen of my hood filled up

with bad wine bad drugs mu shu pork

sick beats what more can I say to you

I open my stylish legs I get my swagger back

let men with gold teeth bow to my tits

and the blisters on my feet I become electric

I'm a patch of grass the stringy roots

you call home or sister if you want

I could scratch your eyes make hip-hop die again

I'm on that grown woman shit before I break

the bottle's neck I pour a little out: you are fallen

Beyoncé Prepares a Will

I have been a pleasure: being
of sound mind and pitch, declare dusk
as long as possible. In accordance with
orange cirrus, let church hats
graze high over my hologram.
Spirit into Gowanus, fingernails
to blog. Let there be black
gold, DJ, finest snack.
Cover the silk of my being.
Promise me, and white teeth
puddling in a drain.
Except as I state, Texas two-step,
electric slide. In the event of
booties to the floor, I want
almond champagne, the lipstick color
you know I want. In the absence of me,
hiss of a leaf folding under your ego.
In the absence of me, smoke and beer.
I am survived by the empire
of imagined bedroom, a pair of diamond
-shaped hips, legacy of
dookie braids and crop top.

The viewing is scheduled.
A vigil will be held in memory of
a prime evening
sweating like ice in a glass.

Please Wait (Or, There Are More Beautiful Things Than Beyoncé)

Please wait to record *Love Jones* at 8:48 Saturday on BET
Until your life is no longer defined by Beyoncé
Ants crawling over fallen leaves and little pieces of dog shit
Empty chicken boxes glowing with the remembrance of grease
There are more beautiful things than Beyoncé: self-awareness,
Leftover mascara in clumps, recognizing a pattern
This is for all the grown women out there
Whose countries hate them and their brothers
Who carry knives in their purses down the street
Maybe they will not get out alive
Maybe they will turn into air or news or brown flower petals
There are more beautiful things than Beyoncé:
Lavender, education, becoming other people,
The fucking sky
It's so overused because no one's sure of it
How it floats with flagrant privilege
And feels it can ask any question
Every day its ego gets bigger and you let that happen
But one day your shit will be unbelievably together
One day you'll care a whole lot you'll always take vitamins
And exercise without bragging and words will fit perfectly
Into your mouth like an olive soaked in gin
The glory of an olive soaked in gin and its smooth smallness

A gloss will snowfall onto your cheeks, the top of your lip
The sidewalks will be the same, evidenced
Combing your records you'll see the past and think OK
Once I was a different kind of person

Funeral for The Black Dog

For the time Beyoncé left Kelly and Michelle

and I left the earth. You came to the greenly

dusted world in my place. You settled in

like a raft of fire ants under the Honey Moon.

For the walls that turned black

with cooked meals and tantrums dear

Morgan, cool out. What do you have to mourn?

In the future it is frigid every day and when

I am awake I deny you like Peter before dawn.

Christ. More than ever I feel

accidental. Your shame swelling in my limbs.

Chamomile and lemon and my mother

cradled you like an infant in a car seat,

patted your stomach until you could sleep said

Baby, imagine but you didn't listen.

Poor Michelle and drawers full of butterflies

and forgotten hash. For the house you built

around your body with broad leaves.

For the men you fucked and swallowed

and fucked and prayed over. You dressed up

in their muscles. For how you are always

still thirsty. For your vision of kingdom.

For great-greats in the croplands and what

their thighs have witnessed. For what chases

us to hiding, steeps us in glass-blown cups.

For the ribs I cracked open for you

to spread yourself up to my clavicle. Your

takeover like a potted plant flooding the room.

For fifteen. For eighteen. For nineteen, twenty-two.

For this hood offering to remember pain

but never to lie down next to it. It is getting late.

I'm sorry. Let me fucking mourn me.

For the diamonds that didn't shake loose.

So What

If a pill comes into bed with me
Melon-colored dawn
Is liquid, grandma's lipstick
Repentance becoming sky
I am tired of coveting
This is where I hang my hat
And kiss myself hello
This is the way it feels to lose
My vision is wind and light
Bottles and men are covered in snow
They touch their lips to a horn
Magical powers are everywhere
Fingernails, post offices
Indoor cactus spines
Everyone gets married to everyone
There is song and dance and drink
Vacant lots confess their flowers
I swallow bold colors because
So what if I have more regrets
Than birthdays I am old
For my age, I am made of water
Why do you get up in the morning

Acknowledgements

Thanks to the editors of the following journals, where versions of these poems first appeared:

Gigantic Sequins: "Lush Life"

Boog City: The Portable Boog Reader 7: "My Vinyl Weighs a Ton," "Ain't Misbehavin'"

Forklift, Ohio: "Untitled While Listening to Drake," "Delicate and Jumpy"

Leveler: "Beyoncé Is Sorry for What She Won't Feel"

Similar: Peaks::: "Let Me Handle My Business, Damn"

Prelude: "Please Wait (Or, There Are More Beautiful Things Than Beyoncé)," "Welcome to the Jungle," "Beyoncé in Third Person"

90s Meg Ryan, Spook: "RoboBeyoncé"

Dusie: "Black Woman with Chicken," "Take a Walk on the Wild Side"

GlitterMOB: "Beyoncé on the Line for Gaga," "White Beyoncé," "Rebirth of Slick"

NOÖ Journal: "Earth, Wind & Fire Reunion Tour 2013"

Big Lucks: "These Are Dangerous Times, Man," "The President's Wife"

Twelfth House: "The Book of Revelation"

Boston Review: "So What," "99 Problems," "The President Has Never Said the Word *Black*"

Poetry Project Newsletter: "Beyoncé Celebrates Black History Month"

Wreck Park: "Another Another Autumn in New York"

The BreakBeat Poets: New American Poetry in the Age of Hip-Hop,
Poetry Magazine: "Let Me Handle My Business, Damn"

Agriculture Reader: "Beyoncé Prepares a Will," "Poem on
Beyoncé's Birthday"

6x6: "We Don't Know When We Were Opened (Or, The Origin of
the Universe)"

Washington Square Review: "Funeral for the Black Dog"

LitHub: "ALL THEY WANT IS MY MONEY MY PUSSY MY
BLOOD"

Paperbag: "The Gospel of Jesus's Wife"

Eleven Eleven: "What Beyoncé Won't Say on a Shrink's Couch"

The Awl: "The Book of Negroes"

H_NGM_N: "Heaven Be a Xanax," "Beyoncé, Touring in Asia,
Breaks Down in a White Tee"

Los Angeles Review of Books: "It's Getting Hot in Here So Take Off
All Your Clothes"

I am wildly grateful for all the hands and hearts that have touched
this book. I am so proud and lucky to call you sisters, husbands,
collaborators, and teachers. Thank you for being the very best
team: Angel Nafis, Jayson Smith, Charif Shanahan, Danez Smith,
Sasha Fletcher, Nate Marshall, Clea Litewka, Vivian Lee, Lizzie
Harris, Willie Fitzgerald, Sam Ross, Jay Deshpande, Ted Meyer,
Adam Fitzgerald, Shanté Cozier, Natalie Eilbert, Molly Rose
Quinn, Matthew Rohrer, Jessica Rankin, Tommy Pico, Leah Feuer,
Rachel Eliza Griffiths, Terrance Hayes, Evie Shockley, D. A. Powell,
Patricia Smith, Saeed Jones, and more and more.

Thanks to Thomas, my twin and mirror. To Mom and Dad:
this one's for you. A special thank you to Mickalene Thomas, a

boundless inspiration to me: it's an honor to be in conversation with you. Eternal gratitude to Dan Kirschen and Tina Wexler (and all the folks at ICM) for being warriors and cheerleaders with endless patience and warmth. Kisses, Xanax, and punk rock to Matthew Dickman, editor and friend. Massive love to Tony Perez, Jakob Vala, and the entire Tin House team for their hustle and enthusiasm. Finally, I bow to my muses: John Coltrane, Carrie Mae Weems, Billie Holiday, Nelly, Drake, Peanut Butter Wolf, W. B. Yeats, Fania All Stars, Digable Planets, Lou Reed, Miles Davis, Barack and Michelle Obama, Jay Z, and of course, Beyoncé Knowles-Carter.